W9-CBL-078

DATE DUE

Placed In
The Media Center
In Recognition Of

Karen Messuri

For Being A
Very Special
Parent Volunteer
at
Aboite Elementary
School

1996-1997

Read All About Dogs

THE WORLD'S SMALLEST DOGS

Barbara J. Patten

The Rourke Corporation, Inc.
Vero Beach, Florida 32964

PHOTO CREDITS
Photos courtesy of Corel

Library of Congress Cataloging-in-Publication Data

Patten, Barbara J., 1951-
    The world's smallest dogs / by Barbara J. Patten.
        p. cm. — (Read all about dogs)
    Includes index.
    Summary: Illustrations and brief text present various breeds of small dogs, including the Japanese Chin, the Chihuahua, Yorkshire and silky terriers, and the Pomeranian.
    ISBN 0-86593-457-6
    1. Toy dogs—Juvenile literature. [1. Toy dogs. 2. Dogs.]
I. Title II. Series: Patten, Barbara J., 1951- Read all about dogs.
SF429.T7P37   1996
636.7'6—dc20   96–19943
                                                                       CIP
                                                                        AC

Printed in the USA

TABLE OF CONTENTS

THE SMALLEST DOGS IN THE WORLD

Ask owners of one of the toy breeds and they may tell you they have big dogs that just happen to live in small bodies.

Dogs in the toy group are tiny. Even when fully grown, most weigh under 15 pounds and are not even 12 inches tall. Some toys look like little models of larger breeds.

Let's read all about the tiniest dogs in the world and their giant personalities.

One of the toy group, the Pekingese stands about 9 inches tall.

JAPANESE CHINS

Weighing under seven pounds, Japanese Chins were once carried in kimono sleeves by Oriental women.

The Japanese chin seems able to sense the difference between a friend and an enemy, which makes it a fine watchdog in spite of its size.

Although not happy around strangers, a Japanese chin is completely devoted to its master.

THE MALTESE

The Maltese, a pretty dog, is perfect for anyone wanting an active pet.

Maltese (mawl TEEZ) look like cuddly stuffed animals, but they are known for their rat-catching ability.

This toy breed has an all-white coat that grows all the way to the floor. Many owners keep the hair in place with a ribbon. Maltese have deep, dark eyes and shiny black noses.

ENGLISH TOY SPANIELS

Hundreds of years ago, **English toy spaniels** (ING glish) (TOY) (SPAN yelz) pranced about the palaces of England. They were loved by kings and queens and were considered very much a part of the Royal Family.

Standing only 10 inches high and weighing under 12 pounds did not discourage these little dogs from hunting woodcocks and other small birds with their masters.

Today, English toy spaniels are seen scampering through backyards or curled up in cozy kitchen corners. They are very affectionate dogs that are content being someone's best friend.

This dog learns the rules of the house quickly, making it a good choice as a family pet.

CHIHUAHUAS

The **Chihuahua** (chi WAH wah) is known as the smallest dog in the world! A Chihuahua may weigh as little as two pounds, fitting easily into a coat pocket. Some have short, smooth coats, others have long, wavy hair.

Don't let the Chihuahua's size fool you. They think they are quite big and act accordingly. Chihuahuas have been known to "run circles around" dogs twice their size and even to attack large dogs to protect their masters.

Chihuahuas have an unusual trait of preferring their own breed over other dogs. Therefore, a chihuahua-only household is best.

Not much higher than an ankle, a Chihuahua can still be a powerhouse.

YORKSHIRE AND SILKY TERRIERS

The **Yorkshire** (YAWRK sheer) and **silky** (SIL kee) terriers are both parts of the toy group because of their small size. Both stand about 9 inches tall.

They are courageous, affectionate, and sometimes a little stubborn. Suspicion of strangers and an ability to locate the slightest noise makes them terrific watchdogs.

A "pony tail" keeps a Yorkie's long hair from blocking its view.

Those pointy little ears hear the slightest noise, making the silky terrier a great watchdog.

Yorkie coats grow so long that they trail on the ground, making the dogs look like they're mounted on wheels as they glide along.

The silky terrier is named for its gray hair that feels as soft as silk. Their coats have a natural part down the back, making the silky look well groomed.

Both of these tiny terriers need lots of grooming to avoid "bad hair days," however.

PUGS

Wrinkles on their heads and curls in their tails make **pugs** (PUGZ) hard to resist. That pushed-in face and those huge round eyes just seem to be begging for a hug.

Pugs probably first lived in China. These sturdy little dogs were taken by ship to England 200 years ago. They soon became walking companions to wealthy English ladies.

Today, pugs are one of the most popular breeds in the toy group. They are friendly dogs that never quite outgrow their funny puppy antics.

Pugs may have coats of black or tan, but both have black faces.

AFFENPINSCHERS

The round head, large eyes, and flyaway hair of an **affenpinscher** (AF en PIN sher) make it look like a monkey. In fact, the affenpinscher has been called "monkey face."

The affenpinscher is an old breed, dating back almost 400 years. Some dog experts believe that an even larger variety of affenpinschers lived in the past.

Although affenpinschers weigh only 7 to 8 pounds, they are known for their courage. They can be real "barkers" and excellent watchdogs.

An affenpinscher is a fearless little dog, especially when protecting its master.

POMERANIANS

Bright-eyed and bushy-tailed, the **Pomeranian** (PAHM uh RAY nee un) is a miniature model of the spitz, a large sled dog. "Poms," as they are called for short, are so tiny at birth that three pups can fit in the palm of your hand.

Pomeranians have a long, thick coat that takes about three years to grow in completely. Petting the straight hair on top may feel rough.

Ready for a bike ride, this "Pom" is looking for someone to pedal.

The German spitz is a giant version of the Pomeranian.

Beneath the harsh top hair is a mass of soft, fluffy hair called an undercoat. This undercoat gives the Pom its bushy look.

Weighing about five pounds, Pomeranians are much too small to pull sleds like their spitz relatives. They can be terrific pets, though, that are quick to bark at strangers, but devoted to their "family."

PETS FROM THE TOY GROUP

Families who own one of the toy breeds will tell you their animal is certainly not a toy.

Like all dogs, these tiny canines need clean water, healthy food, medical care, and a warm, safe place to sleep. Many of the toy breeds require lots of regular combing and brushing to keep their coats free of painful tangles.

Toys are famous for their ability to understand words and voice tone. Speak as kindly to your canine friends as you speak to human ones.

Like all pups, these English toy spaniels need lots of rest.

GLOSSARY

affenpinscher (AF en PIN sher) — a small dog with wiry, shaggy hair and a "beard"

canine (KAY nyn) — of or about dogs; like a dog

Chihuahua (chi WAH wah) — known as the smallest dog in the world, has pointed ears and smooth coat

English toy spaniel (ING glish) (TOY) (SPAN yel) — a dog with round head, short turned-up nose, thick wavy coat, and mane

Maltese (mawl TEEZ) — a toy breed with a long, silky white coat

Pomeranian (PAHM uh RAY nee un) — a silky dog with pointed ears, foxlike face, and hairy tail curling over its back

pug (PUG) — a sturdy dog with snub nose, wrinkled face, square body, short smooth hair, and curled tail

silky terrier (SIL kee) (TER ee er) — a small active breed once used for driving game out of the ground

Yorkshire terrier (YAWRK sheer) (TER ee er) — a breed with long, silky, blue-gray coat

A training crate keeps this Yorkshire terrier safe and out of trouble.

INDEX